PIANO · VOCAL · CHORDS

# Top Movie Hits

MW00803174

Alfred Publishing Co., Inc.
16320 Roscoe Blvd., Suite 100
P.O. Box 10003
Van Nuys, CA 91410-0003
alfred.com

ISBN-10: 0-7390-5637-9
ISBN-13: 978-0-7390-5637-0

Cover photographs:
Nightlife VIP © istockphoto.com/jgroup
Cheering Crowd Under Stars © istockphoto.com/nopow

# CONTENTS

*(from "August Rush")*

# AUGUST RUSH

(Piano Suite)

Composed by
MARK MANCINA
*Arranged by DAVE METZGER*

**Gently ( ♩. = 54)**
*"Main Theme"*

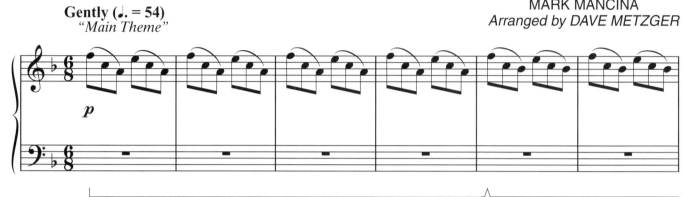

**Delicately** (♩ = 80)

*"August's Theme"*

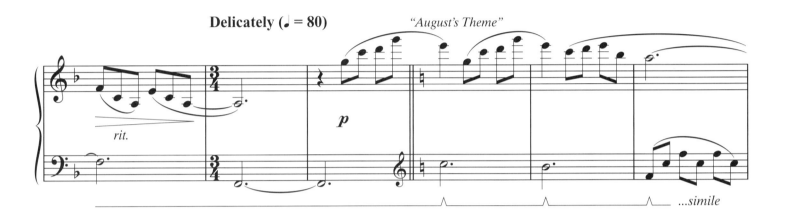

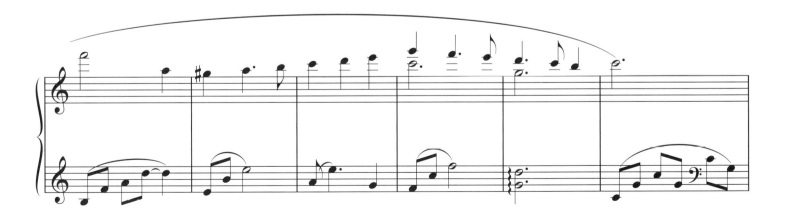

*(a bit more deliberately)*

*"Parents Theme"*

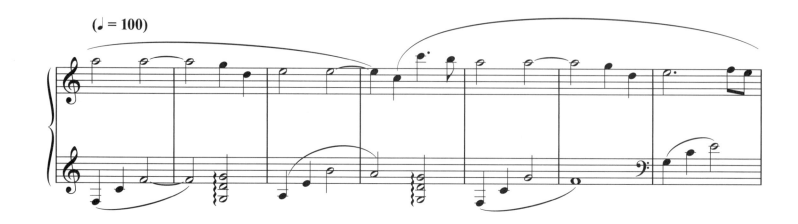

"August's Rhapsody"

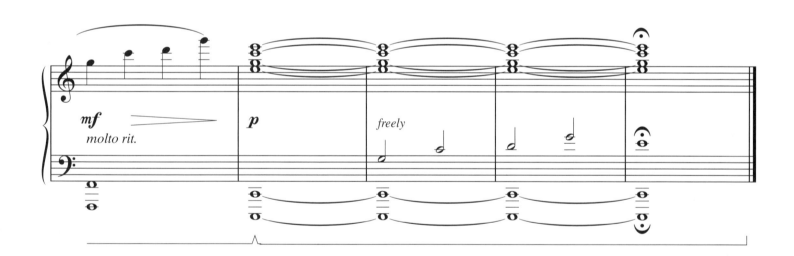

*(from "The Corpse Bride")*

# CORPSE BRIDE (MAIN TITLE)

Music by
DANNY ELFMAN

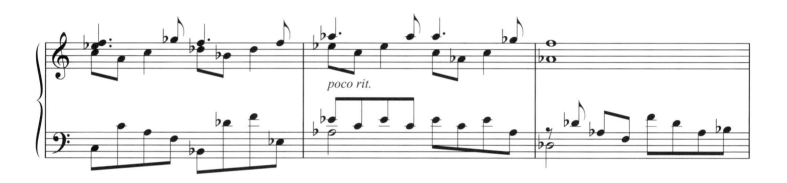

Corpse Bride (Main Title) - 3 - 1

*(from "Once")*

# FALLING SLOWLY

Words and Music by
GLEN HANSARD and
MARKETA IRGLOVA

**Slowly** ♩ = 69

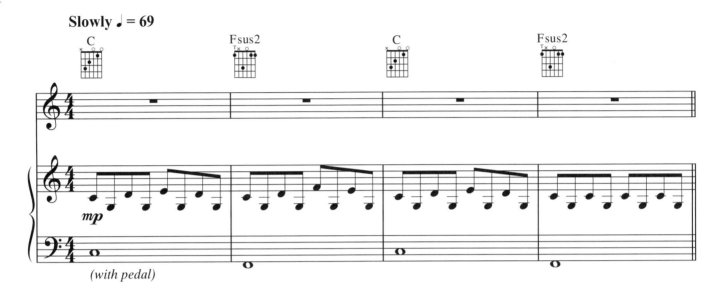

(with pedal)

*Verse 1:*

1. I don't know you, but I want you all the more for that.

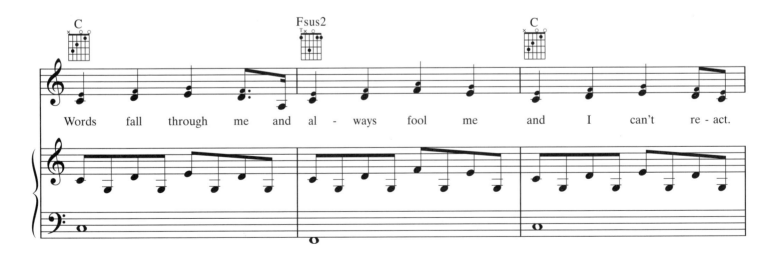

Words fall through me and al-ways fool me and I can't re-act.

Falling Slowly - 6 - 1

(Strings)

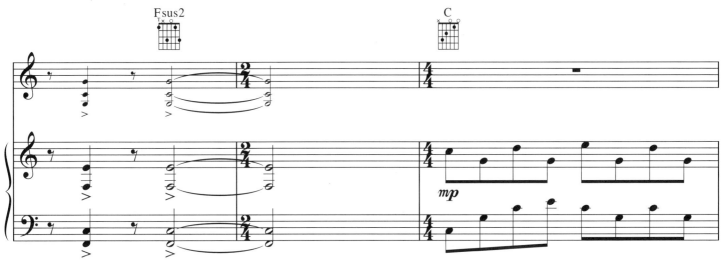

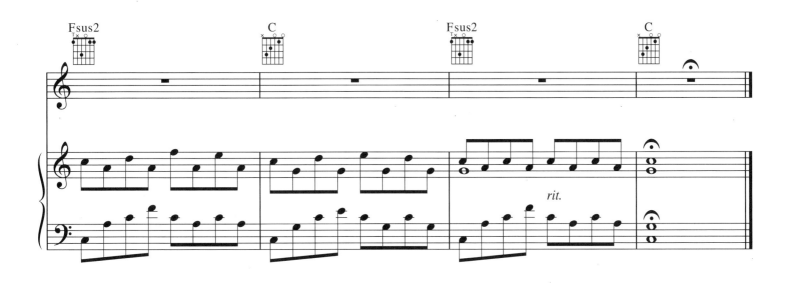

*(from "Harry Potter and the Sorcerer's Stone")*

# HEDWIG'S THEME

Music by
**JOHN WILLIAMS**

Hedwig's Theme - 5 - 1

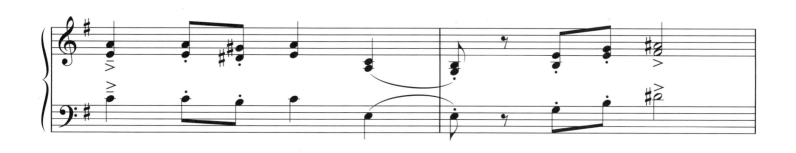

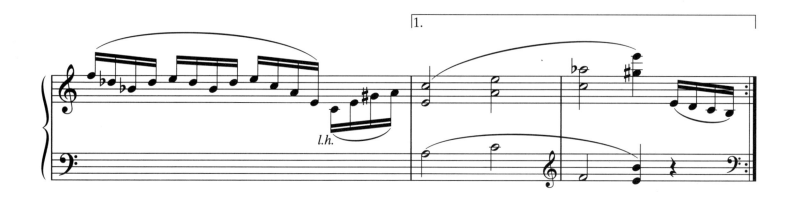

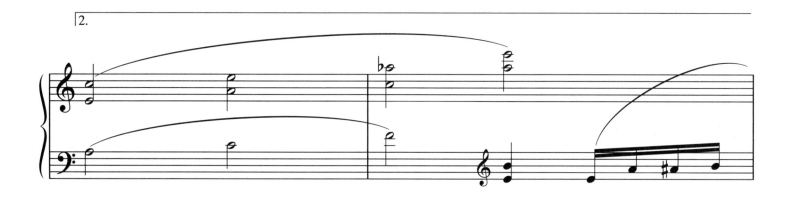

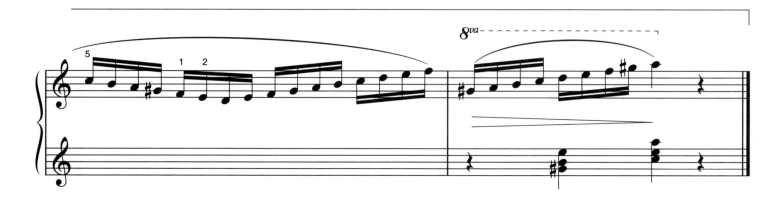

*(from "The Lord of the Rings: The Fellowship of the Ring")*

# IN DREAMS

*(featured in "The Breaking of the Fellowship")*

Words and Music by
FRAN WALSH and
HOWARD SHORE

In Dreams - 3 - 1

*(from "The Notebook")*
# THE NOTEBOOK
## (Main Title)

Written by
AARON ZIGMAN

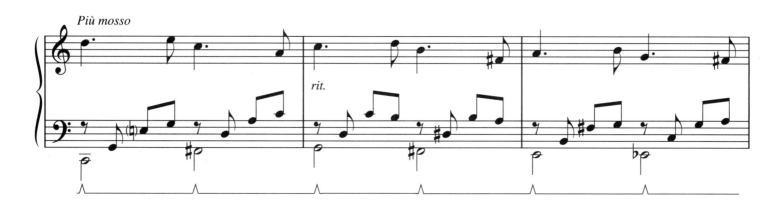

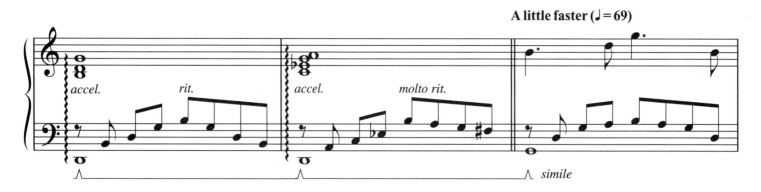

The Notebook - 3 - 1

28

(from "Music & Lyrics")

# WAY BACK INTO LOVE

Words and Music by
ADAM SCHLESINGER

Way Back Into Love - 7 - 1

*(from "Indiana Jones and the Kingdom of the Crystal Skull")*

# RAIDERS MARCH

Music by
**JOHN WILLIAMS**

**March (♩ = 120)**

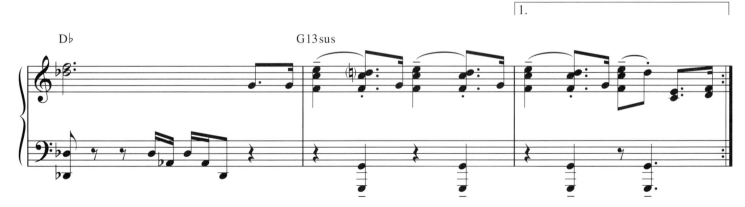

Raiders March - 4 - 1

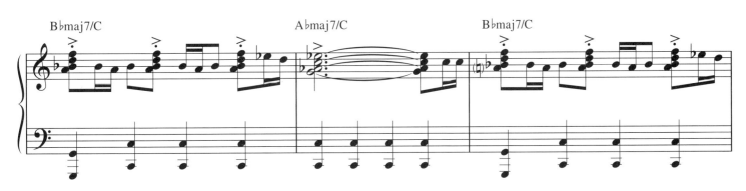

Raiders March - 4 - 2

*(from "Star Wars")*

# STAR WARS
(Main Title)

Music by
**JOHN WILLIAMS**

**Majestically, steady march (♩ = 108)**

Star Wars - 4 - 1

# THEME FROM "SUPERMAN"

Music by
**JOHN WILLIAMS**

Theme From "Superman" - 4 - 1

Theme From "Superman" - 4 - 4